I0606242

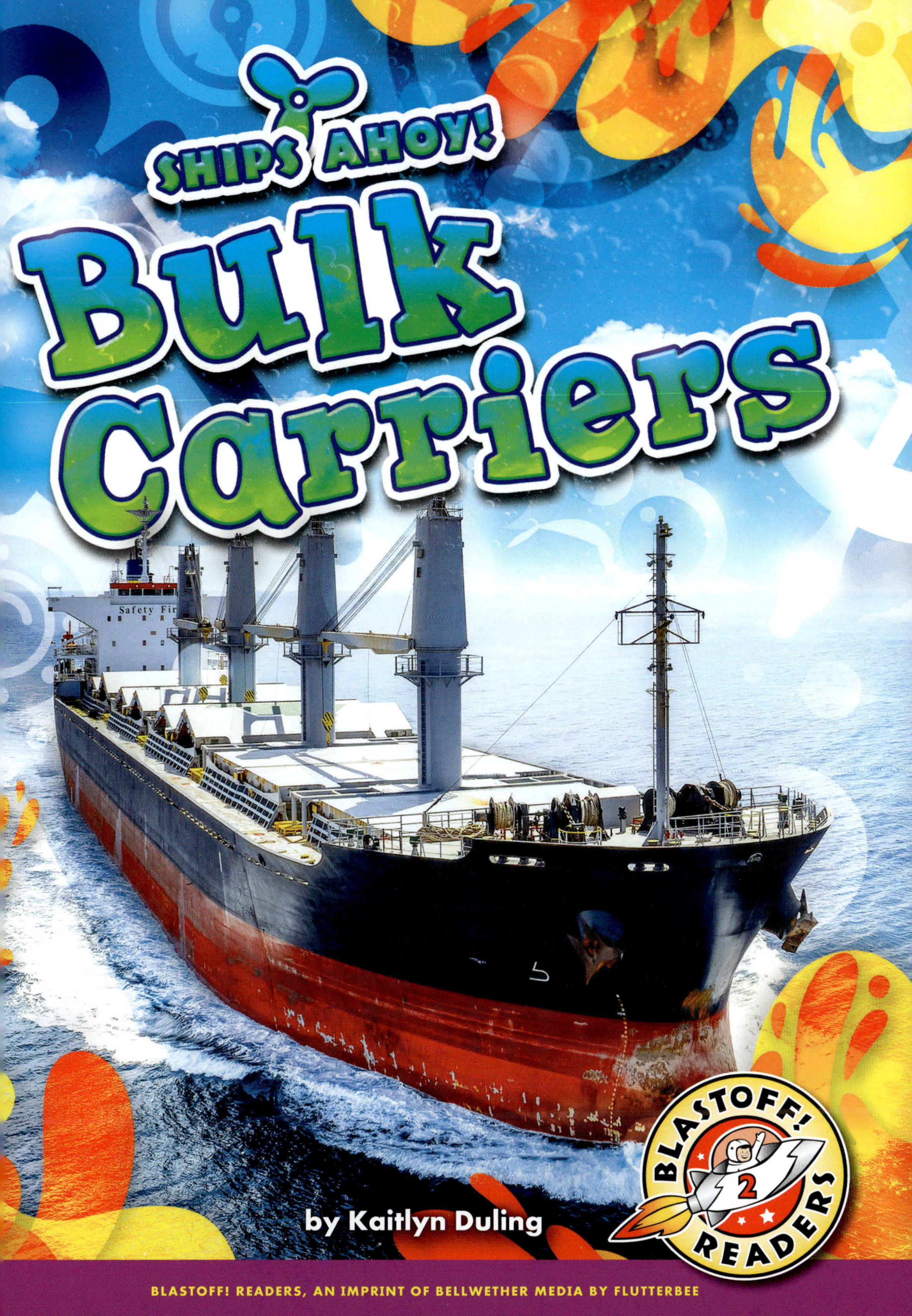
SHIPS AHOY!
Bulk Carriers
by Kaitlyn Duling
BLASTOFF! 2 READERS
BLASTOFF! READERS, AN IMPRINT OF BELLWETHER MEDIA BY FLUTTERBEE

Blastoff! Readers are carefully developed by literacy experts to build reading stamina and move students toward fluency by combining standards-based content with developmentally appropriate text.

LEVELS

Level 1 provides the most support through repetition of high-frequency words, light text, predictable sentence patterns, and strong visual support.

Level 2 offers early readers a bit more challenge through varied sentences, increased text load, and text-supportive special features.

Level 3 advances early-fluent readers toward fluency through increased text load, less reliance on photos, advancing concepts, longer sentences, and more complex special features.

★ **Blastoff! Universe**

Reading Level

Grade K

Grades 1–3

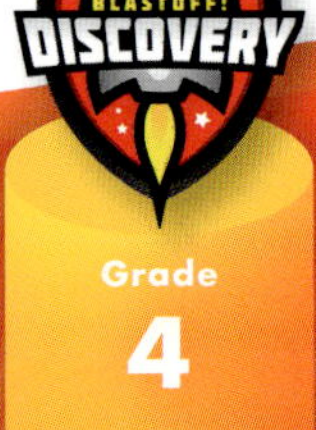

Grade 4

This edition first published in 2026 by Bellwether Media, Inc.

For information regarding permission, write to Bellwether Media, Inc., Attention: Permissions Department, 3500 American Blvd W, Suite 150, Bloomington, MN 55431.

Library of Congress Cataloging-in-Publication Data is available at www.loc.gov or upon request from the publisher.

ISBN: 9798893047998 (hardcover)
ISBN: 9798893048995 (ebook)

Editor: Kieran Downs   Designer: Jennifer Bowyer

Printed in the United States of America, North Mankato, MN.

Table of Contents

What Are Bulk Carriers?

Bulk carriers are large ships. They carry **cargo** long distances.

Their cargo is loose. They carry grain, coal, and salt. Some carry iron **ore**.

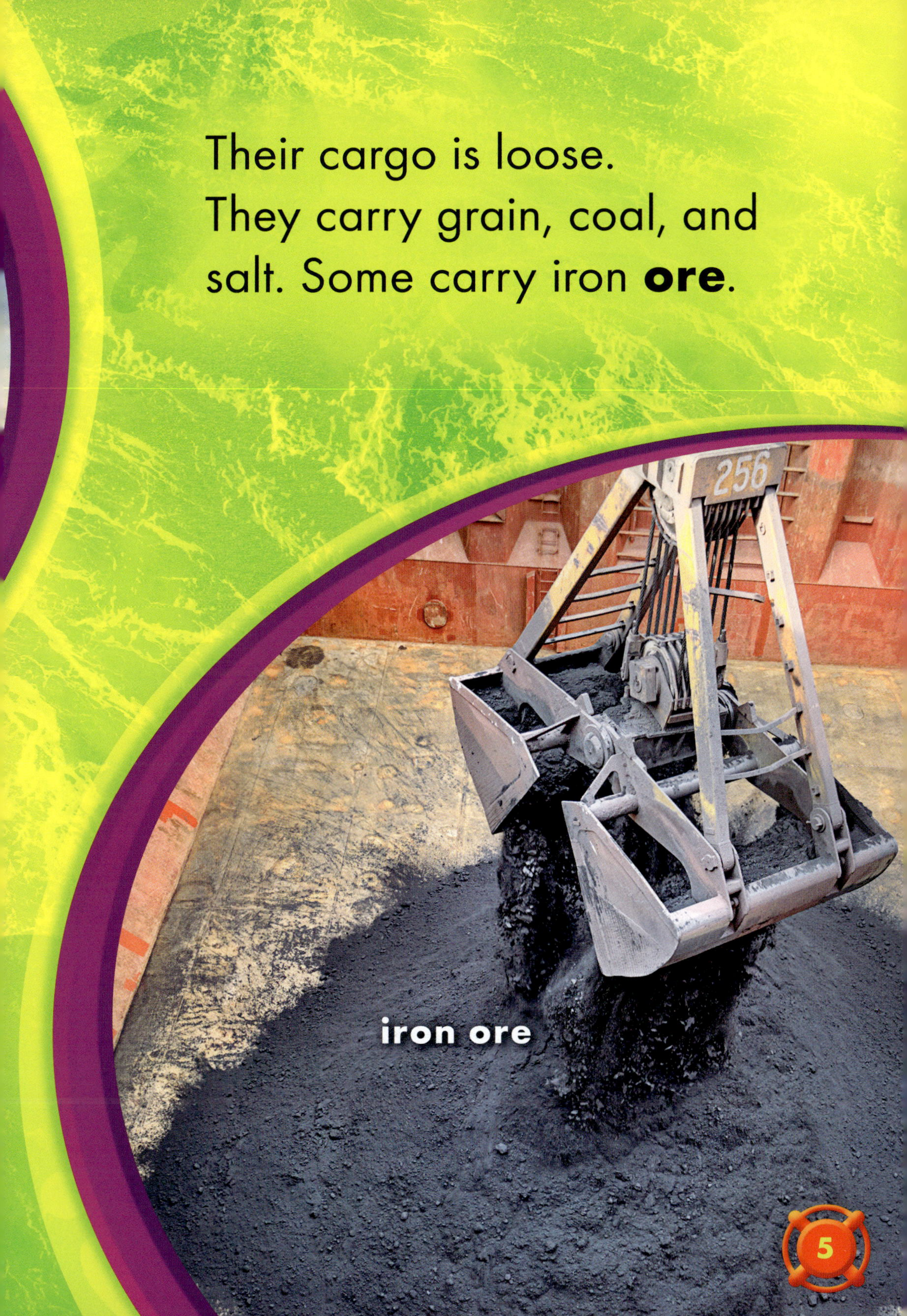

iron ore

Bulk carriers have strong **hulls**. They protect the ship and its cargo.

Parts of a Bulk Carrier

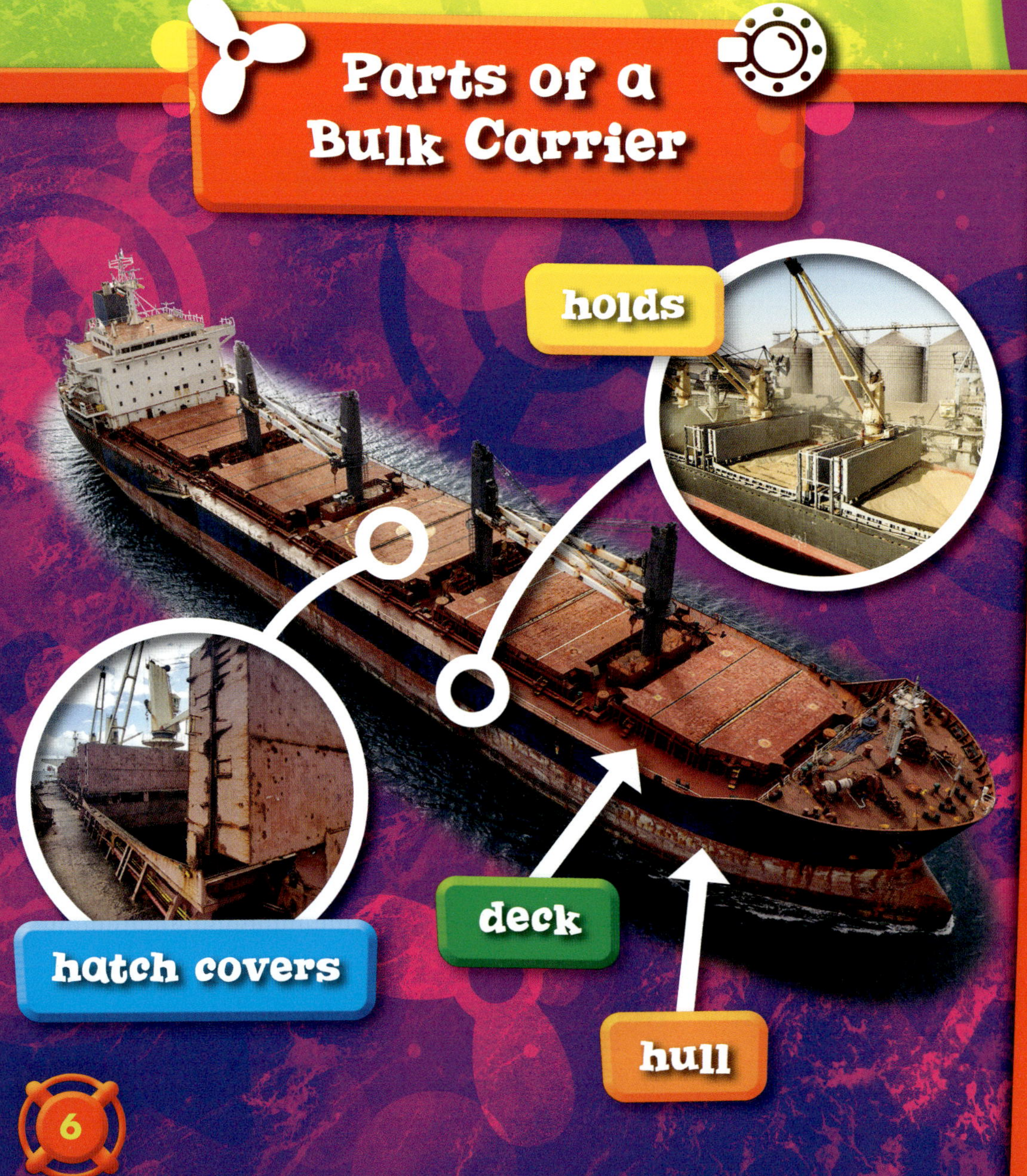

hatch covers

hold

Cargo is stored in **holds**. Hatch covers keep water out of the holds.

Bulk carriers have long, flat **decks**. Some have **cranes**.

Cranes are used to load and unload cargo in the **port**.

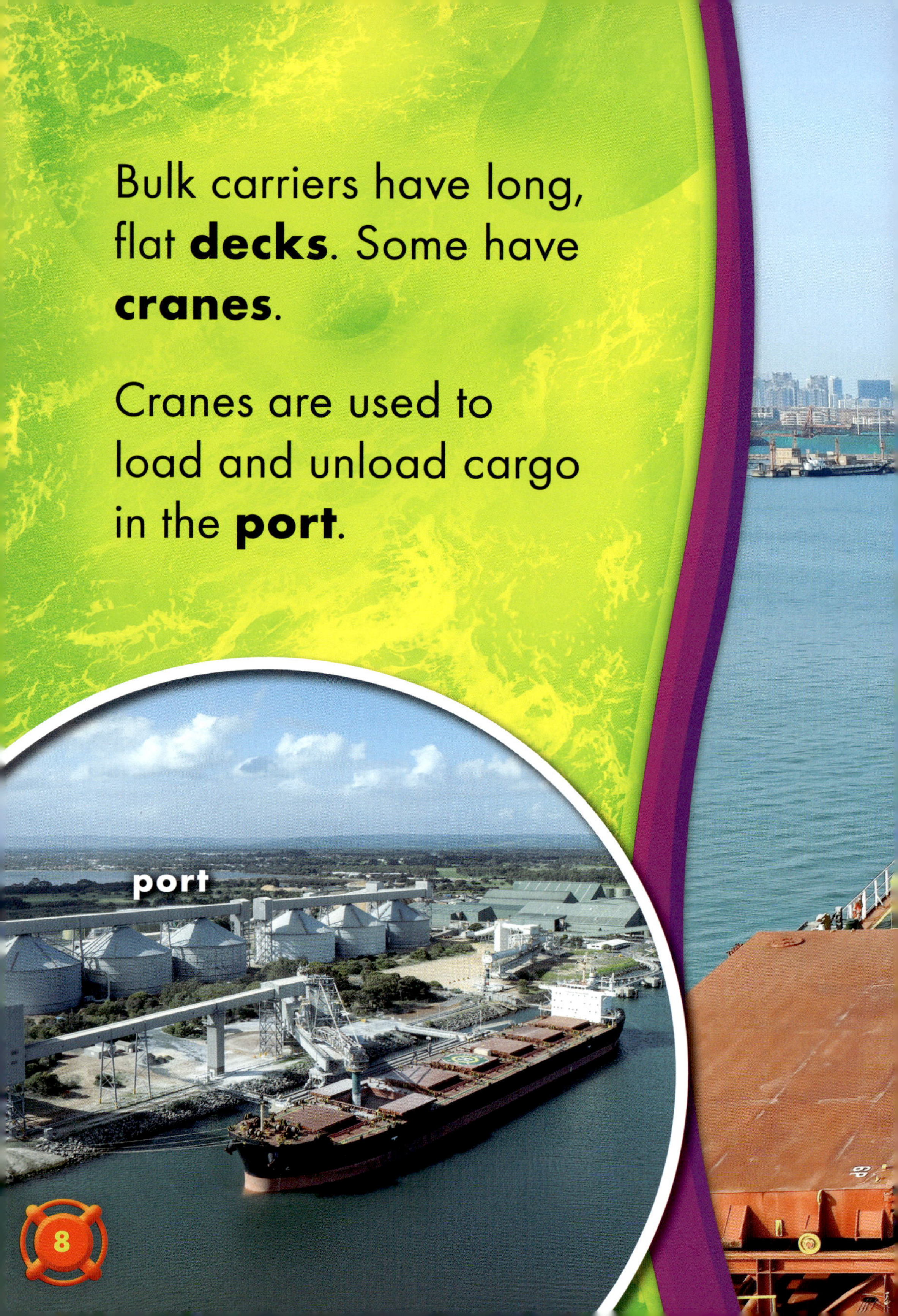

crane
deck

Types of Bulk Carriers

mini bulk carrier

Handymax carrier

very large ore carrier (VLOC)

Bulk carriers come in many sizes. Mini bulk carriers are the smallest.

Very large ore carriers (VLOC) are the biggest. **Handymax** carriers can go into smaller ports.

Massive Movers

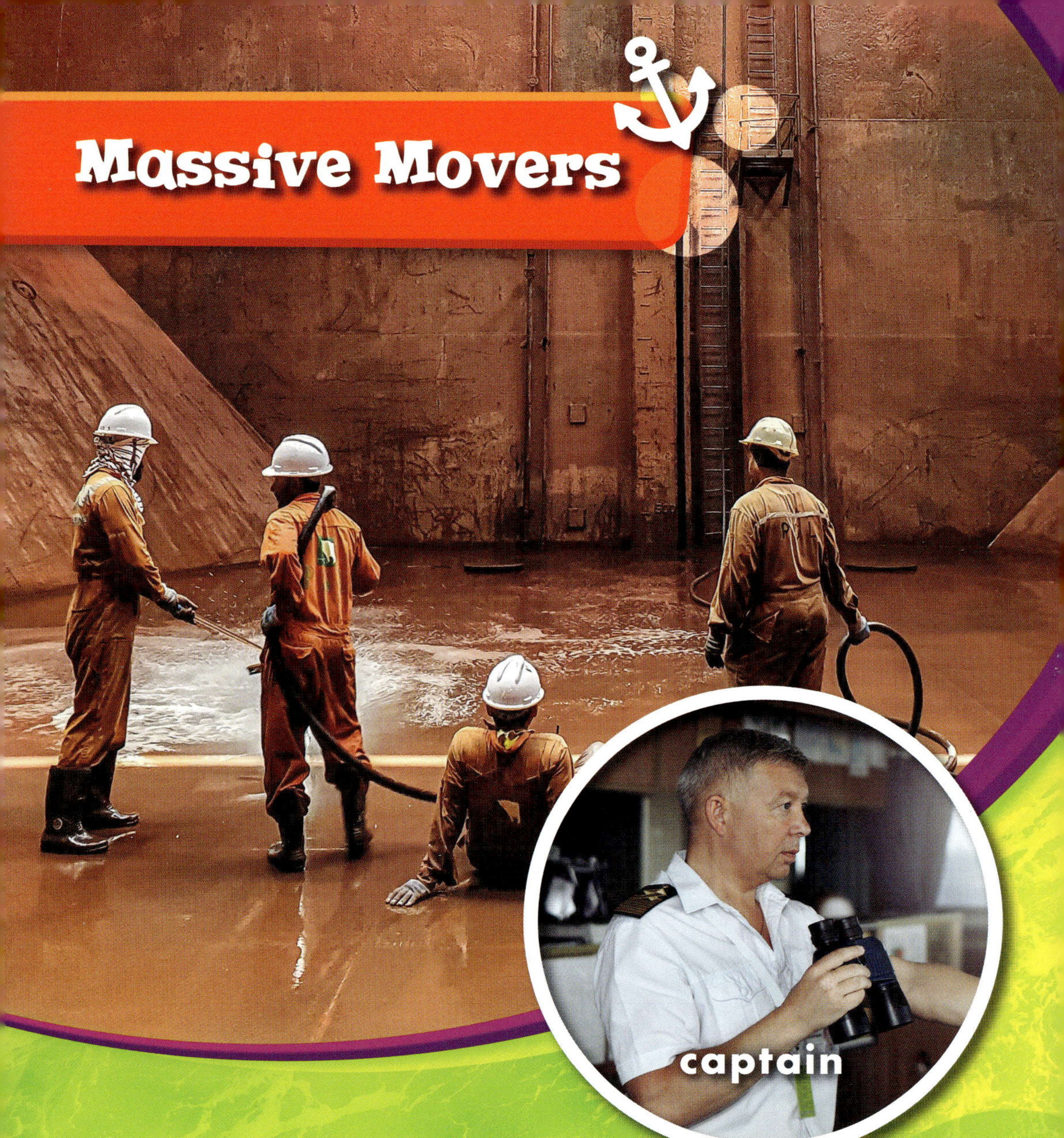

captain

There are around 20 crew members on each bulk carrier. The captain controls the ship.

Crew members clean the holds. They also load the cargo.

Ship Stats

Pacific Flourish

Size 1,188 feet (362 meters) long; 213 feet (65 meters) wide

Type very large ore carrier (VLOC)

Speed 14 knots (16 miles or 28 kilometers per hour)

Purpose moves large amounts of rocks and iron ore

The ship's mates plan the loading and unloading of the ship.

Cargo can be heavy. It can take many hours for crew members to load and unload.

Self-unloading ships use **conveyor belts**. These ships need fewer crew members to unload.

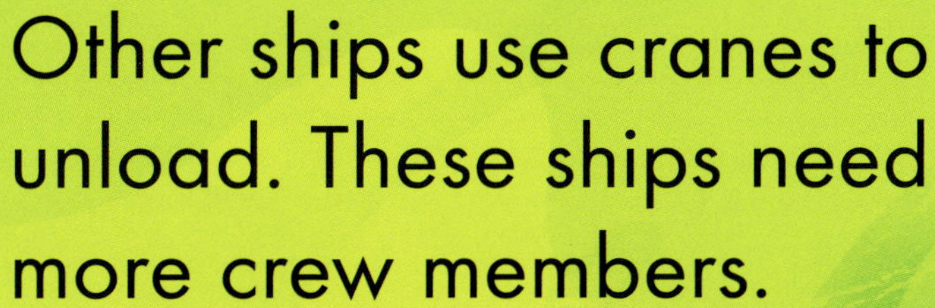

Other ships use cranes to unload. These ships need more crew members.

Unloading a Self-Unloading Bulk Carrier

4 The cargo is moved to another conveyer belt and unloaded.

1 Gates open at the bottom of the cargo hold.

2 Cargo falls onto a conveyor belt.

3 A special elevator moves the cargo up to the deck.

The ship's **engine** sends power to a **propeller**.

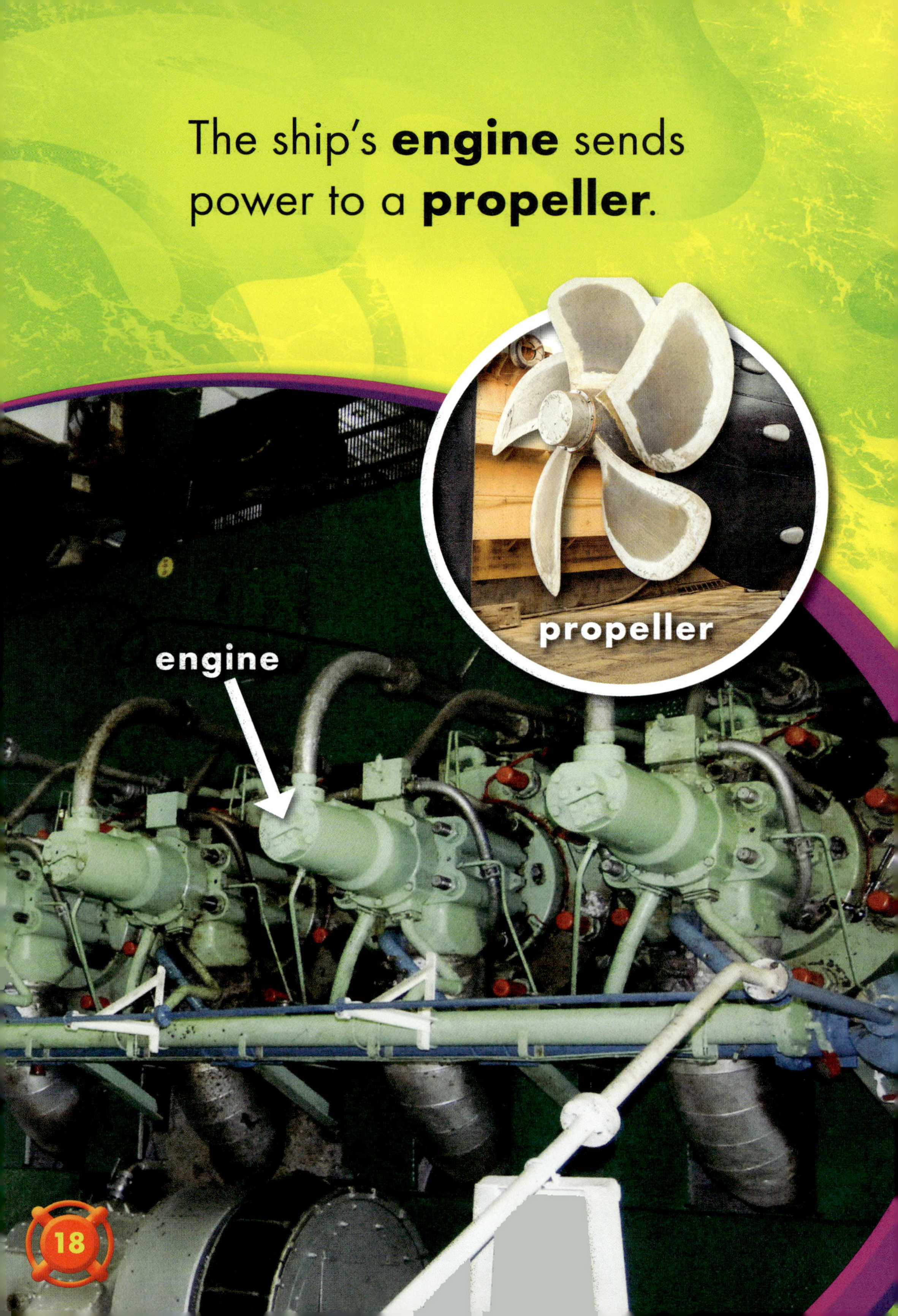

Bulk carriers can travel around 15 **knots** (17 miles or 27 kilometers per hour).

Carry On!

Bulk carriers move important cargo! Their cargo helps feed and house people around the world.

They carry cargo all over the globe!

M S C

Glossary

cargo—goods carried by a ship

conveyor belts—devices that move things from one place to another

cranes—machines used to lift and move heavy loads

decks—flat parts on the top of a ship

engine—a machine with moving parts that changes power into motion

Handymax—a kind of bulk carrier that can move cargo into smaller ports

holds—large areas below a ship's deck that are used to store cargo

hulls—the main bodies of ships

knots—units of measurement used to explain the speed of a ship

ore—a natural material that contains a valuable metal

port—a place where ships load and unload

propeller—a part of a ship that has blades that spin; propellers help a ship move through water.

To Learn More

AT THE LIBRARY

Duling, Kaitlyn. *Container Ships.* Minneapolis, Minn.: Bellwether Media, 2026.

Rathburn, Betsy. *A Ship's Day.* Minneapolis, Minn.: Bellwether Media, 2024.

Walker, Alan. *Ships Go!* New York, N.Y.: Crabtree Publishing Company, 2023.

ON THE WEB

FACTSURFER

Factsurfer.com gives you a safe, fun way to find more information.

1. Go to www.factsurfer.com.
2. Enter "bulk carriers" into the search box and click 🔍.
3. Select your book cover to see a list of related content.

Index

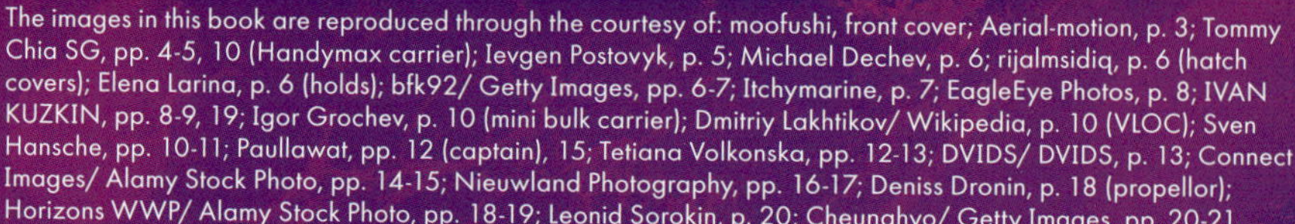

The images in this book are reproduced through the courtesy of: moofushi, front cover; Aerial-motion, p. 3; Tommy Chia SG, pp. 4-5, 10 (Handymax carrier); Ievgen Postovyk, p. 5; Michael Dechev, p. 6; rijalmsidiq, p. 6 (hatch covers); Elena Larina, p. 6 (holds); bfk92/ Getty Images, pp. 6-7; Itchymarine, p. 7; EagleEye Photos, p. 8; IVAN KUZKIN, pp. 8-9, 19; Igor Grochev, p. 10 (mini bulk carrier); Dmitriy Lakhtikov/ Wikipedia, p. 10 (VLOC); Sven Hansche, pp. 10-11; Paullawat, pp. 12 (captain), 15; Tetiana Volkonska, pp. 12-13; DVIDS/ DVIDS, p. 13; Connect Images/ Alamy Stock Photo, pp. 14-15; Nieuwland Photography, pp. 16-17; Deniss Dronin, p. 18 (propellor); Horizons WWP/ Alamy Stock Photo, pp. 18-19; Leonid Sorokin, p. 20; Cheunghyo/ Getty Images, pp. 20-21.